TIME
FOR KIDS

Batter Up!
History of
Baseball

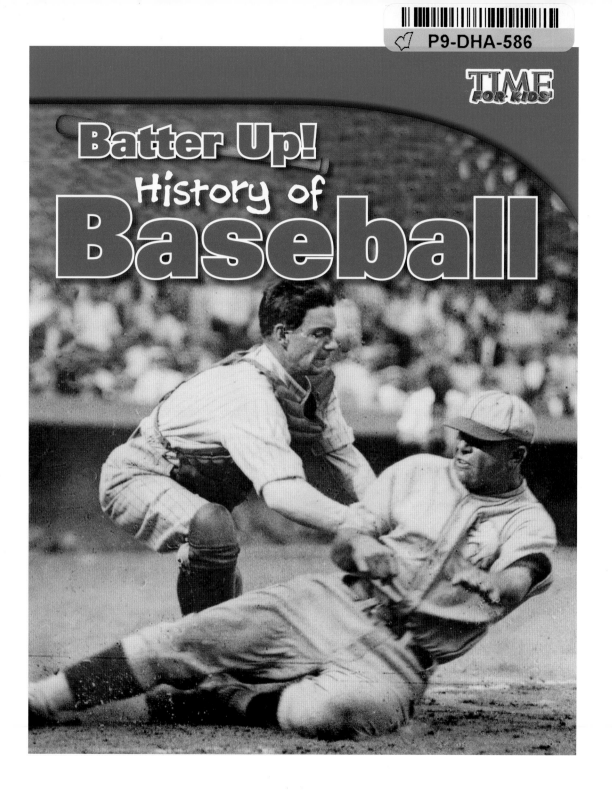

Dona Herweck Rice

Consultant

Timothy Rasinski, Ph.D.
Kent State University

Publishing Credits

Dona Herweck Rice, *Editor-in-Chief*

Robin Erickson, *Production Director*

Lee Aucoin, *Creative Director*

Conni Medina, M.A.Ed., *Editorial Director*

Jamey Acosta, *Editor*

Heidi Kellenberger, *Editor*

Lexa Hoang, *Designer*

Lesley Palmer, *Designer*

Stephanie Reid, *Photo Editor*

Rachelle Cracchiolo, M.S.Ed., *Publisher*

Based on writing from *TIME For Kids*.

TIME For Kids and the *TIME For Kids* logo are registered trademarks of TIME Inc. Used under license.

Teacher Created Materials

5301 Oceanus Drive
Huntington Beach, CA 92649-1030
http://www.tcmpub.com

ISBN 978-1-4333-3679-9

© 2012 Teacher Created Materials, Inc.

Table of Contents

In the Big Inning

Take a bat, a ball, a mitt, and a warm summer day. Put them all together, and you've got the great game of baseball!

Big Inning?

The chapter title "In the Big Inning" is a **pun**. It sounds like "In the Beginning," but it uses a section of a baseball game—an inning—to make a joke. There are nine innings in a baseball game.

But baseball hasn't always existed. Who invented the game? Who wrote the rules? Who wore the first uniform and glove? Who hit the first home run, and when was the first World Series played? We know the answers to some of these things. Others we don't know, and for some we can only make a guess.

National Pastime

Baseball is called America's *national pastime.* That is because it is one of the most popular sports in the United States, both to play and to watch.

children playing Little League baseball

6

As far as we know, games with sticks, balls, and bases have been played for centuries. Baseball seems to have grown naturally from these games. It wasn't invented by just one person. Many people think that it came from the British games **rounders** and **cricket**. As early as the 1700s, people were playing some form of these games.

adults playing professional cricket

Before Baseball

Cricket is a game with many similarities to baseball. Cricket is played outside with 11 players on each team. They use bats, a ball, and wickets, which are stick-like targets.

People today usually think that Abner Doubleday invented baseball. It's no wonder. After Doubleday died, a man named Abner Graves claimed he saw Doubleday invent the game in 1839. He said that Doubleday made the first baseball diamond in a field in Cooperstown, New York.

Abner Doubleday

Doubleday may not have invented baseball, but he was a great man nonetheless. After graduating from West Point in 1842, he immediately began a distinguished military career. Eventually, he became an honored major general.

Abner Doubleday
(1819–1893)

NEW YORK

COOPERSTOWN

WEST POINT

Even though Abner Doubleday didn't invent baseball there, Cooperstown is still considered to be baseball's hometown.

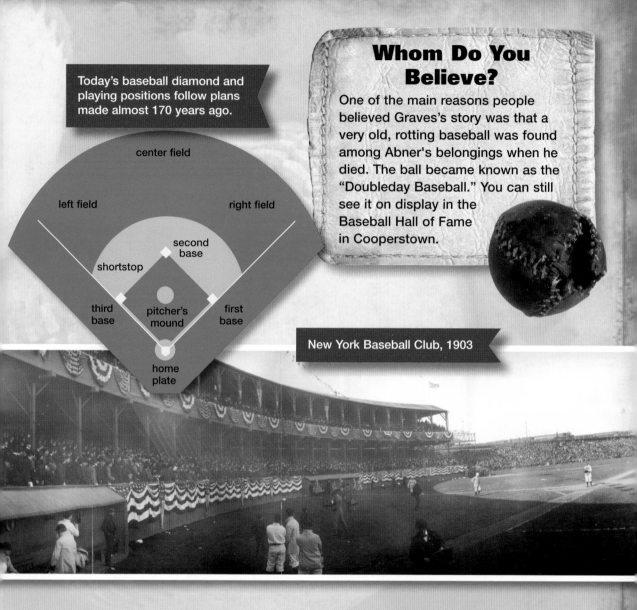

Today's baseball diamond and playing positions follow plans made almost 170 years ago.

center field

left field

right field

second base

shortstop

third base

pitcher's mound

first base

home plate

Whom Do You Believe?

One of the main reasons people believed Graves's story was that a very old, rotting baseball was found among Abner's belongings when he died. The ball became known as the "Doubleday Baseball." You can still see it on display in the Baseball Hall of Fame in Cooperstown.

New York Baseball Club, 1903

The trouble is, Doubleday was a **cadet** at West Point military academy in 1839. He was not in Cooperstown, and he didn't have time for baseball. Also, Doubleday left many journals when he died. He doesn't mention baseball in any of them. A 1911 encyclopedia article about Doubleday doesn't mention baseball either.

A man named Alexander Cartwright is the one who probably did all the things Doubleday was given credit for.

Of course, to be a real game that everyone can play in the same way wherever they go, there must be **standard** rules. In 1845, an **amateur** team in New York decided to write the rules of baseball. And that's where the rest of baseball's history begins.

Children around the world enjoy playing baseball and games very similar to it.

Baseball's First Mention

In literature, an early mention of baseball can be found in a classic novel by Jane Austen called *Northanger Abbey*. It was written in 1798 but not published until 1817. The heroine of the novel, Catherine Morland, is said to have enjoyed "cricket, baseball, [and] riding on horseback" when she was a girl.

How Do We Know?

A New York City librarian named Robert Henderson did a lot to prove Cartwright was an inventor of baseball. He tells all about Cartwright's work in his 1947 book, *Bat, Ball and Bishop*. On June 3, 1953, the United States Congress used Henderson's research to name Cartwright as baseball's founder instead of Abner Doubleday.

Alexander Cartwright

Around the world, people use all different-size balls and bats to play baseball.

The Rules

In 1842, a group called the New York Knickerbockers started getting together to play baseball. They were young **professionals** who liked to play the game. In 1845, they formed the Knickerbocker Baseball Club and decided to write the rules for baseball. Led by Daniel L. "Doc" Adams, they wrote down the rules. This allowed everyone who played baseball to play the game in the same way.

Over time, the rules for baseball have changed a bit. They're still changing! Here and on the next few pages are some of the highlights of baseball's changing rules.

The New York Knickerbockers don't exist today, but without the team's contributions to baseball, today's teams might not exist either.

Rules Time Line

1845	1857	1860	1864	1864	1870	1876
The player must hold the ball when tagging a runner out. (Before this rule, the runner was out if struck by a thrown ball.)	A game is nine innings. The winning team has the most runs at the end of nine innings.	**Foul** lines are marked with whitewash.	A runner must touch all the bases when circling them.	In order to be out, a hit ball must be caught with no bounces.	A runner may overrun first base.	An umpire can ask for the crowds' or players' opinions if he can't see a play.

Cartwright and the Knickerbockers

Alexander Cartwright was part of the Knickerbocker committee that wrote the rules of baseball. The name Knickerbocker was Cartwright's suggestion, too. He took it from the Knickerbocker Engine Company for which he had been a volunteer fireman.

The First Rules

The earliest rules for baseball included two teams of nine players each. They played on a baseball square with a base at each corner. The batter's base was called *home*. Bats could be any size or shape. The batter was out with three **strikes** or if the hit ball was caught with one or no bounces. There were three outs for each side in an inning. Runners could be tagged or **forced out**. Each team got an equal number of turns at bat. The winning team was the first to score 21 *aces*, the original name for **runs**. Later, an **umpire** was named as the judge during play.

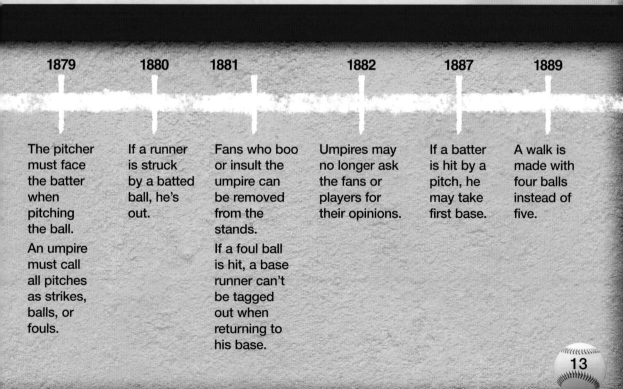

1879	1880	1881	1882	1887	1889
The pitcher must face the batter when pitching the ball. An umpire must call all pitches as strikes, balls, or fouls.	If a runner is struck by a batted ball, he's out.	Fans who boo or insult the umpire can be removed from the stands. If a foul ball is hit, a base runner can't be tagged out when returning to his base.	Umpires may no longer ask the fans or players for their opinions.	If a batter is hit by a pitch, he may take first base.	A walk is made with four balls instead of five.

13

The rules of baseball are still changing today. Safety is very important, so officials study new bats, balls, and helmets to make sure they are safe. They also work hard to make the game fair to all players.

First Game

Under the new rules, the first recorded game of baseball was played on October 6, 1845. Both teams were made up of members of the Knickerbockers. The first real baseball game played by opposing teams took place on June 19, 1846. The New York Knickerbockers played against the New York Club. The Knickerbockers lost 23–1.

Rules Time Line

1891	1895	1898	1901	1908	1910
Player substitutions may be made, but a substituted player may not return to the game.	The bat must be round and made of wood. The umpire can call off a game if the fans are disorderly. In that case, the visiting team wins, 9-0.	Runners may **steal** bases. If a pitcher makes a motion to throw in the direction of a base, he must actually throw the ball or be charged with a **balk**.	The first two fouls a batter hits are called *strikes*.	Pitchers may not scuff or dirty a new ball.	Baseballs have cork centers.

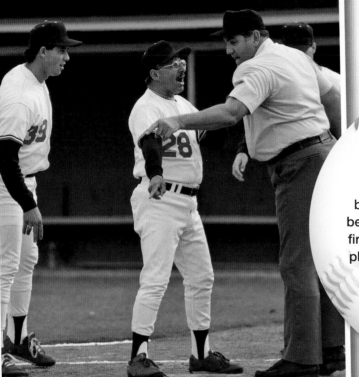

"Hey, Ump!"

One of the many traditions of baseball seems to be arguments between players and umpires. The first recorded argument between a player and an umpire was in 1846. Who won? The umpire did, of course.

1920	1949	1952	1959	1968	1974
A runner may not run the bases backwards in order to confuse the other team.	On December 21st, a new rule book is issued. The rules are mainly the same, but the unclear parts are corrected.	Daily games have four umpires.	When a new ballpark is built, its outfield fence must be a minimum number of feet from the diamond.	The pitcher's mound is 10 inches above home plate and the base lines.	A relief pitcher is given the save if he protects a lead.

Dressed to Play Ball

Today, an important part of baseball is the uniform. As you can see, uniforms have changed over time. The first uniforms were worn by the Knickerbockers in 1849. They were blue and white and made of wool.

Baseball caps were first made of straw. In the 1850s, the Knickerbockers chose a wool hat with a bill to protect the player's eyes from bright sunlight.

1901
Cy Young

1907
Harry Wright

1940
Ted Williams

Retired Numbers

Having his number retired by a team is one of the greatest honors a player can receive. That means that no other player for the team will ever wear that number.

It wasn't until 1870 that a catcher's glove was added to the game. In 1962, a standard size was set for gloves.

The first numbers were added to uniforms in 1907 for the Reading Red Roses of Pennsylvania. This was to help fans identify the players.

Spikes, called *cleats*, were added to baseball shoes in the late 1860s. In 1976, rules for spikes were added to the official rulebook.

Getting hit by a ball can be dangerous, so in 1971, the leagues agreed that all players must wear helmets at bat. In 1988, catchers were told to do the same.

2010
Ryan Lavarnway

Colors and Fabrics

In the early days of baseball, bright red was not worn by teams who wanted to think of themselves as gentlemanly and upper class. That is also why they chose wool for their uniforms. Although cotton was less expensive and more comfortable, it was used only for worker's clothing in the mid-nineteenth century, not the clothes of "respectable" classes.

Rally Cap

When players turn their caps inside out, it's called a *rally cap*. Rally caps are worn when teams are making a comeback to win a game.

Leagues of Their Own

While baseball has always been a fun sport, it hasn't always been a fair sport for everyone. For many years, African Americans were kept from playing in the professional leagues. Women only played for a short time in a professional league of their own.

the All-American Girls Professional Baseball League posing for a portrait in their uniforms in 1945

Women in the All-American Girls league had to wear short dresses when they played. They had to run, jump, catch, and slide while wearing these impractical uniforms. People thought it wouldn't be ladylike if the women wore shorts or pants.

Women played professional baseball from 1943 until 1954. The All-American Girls Professional Baseball League began during World War II when many men were away fighting the war. The women were tough, and the league became popular. During its existence, more than 600 women athletes played professional baseball. The league fell apart when its management changed. Today there is a push to bring women back to professional baseball.

Today's Leagues

Baseball has become very popular in Latin America. It took many years for Latino players like Roberto Clemente to be accepted in the United States. And in the 1980s there was an explosion of Latino players into the major leagues. Today many of the best players are from Latin America.

In the earliest days of baseball, some black and white players played together. But, in the 1890s, an unwritten agreement spread through the leagues to keep all African American players out. The main reasons for this were hate and fear. There were, of course, many African American athletes who were among the best baseball players of the time. The Negro National League was formed so they could play.

All-black teams had started in the 1880s. In the early 1900s, they became more successful. Finally, in the 1920s, Andrew "Rube" Foster organized the Negro National League. Other African American leagues followed.

Moses "Fleetwood" Walker was the first black player in the major leagues before black players were kept out.

Andrew "Rube" Foster was the force behind the Negro National League created in 1920.

Big Business

During their best times, the black leagues were some of the largest and most successful businesses owned by African Americans.

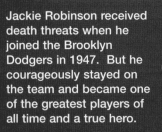

Jackie Robinson received death threats when he joined the Brooklyn Dodgers in 1947. But he courageously stayed on the team and became one of the greatest players of all time and a true hero.

The End of the Leagues

After Robinson, more and more black players joined the major leagues. Finally, the black leagues lost all of their best players. The last black league closed in 1962.

Black leagues continued successfully until the color **barrier** in baseball was finally broken. That happened when Jackie Robinson, a great player in the black leagues, began playing for the Brooklyn Dodgers in 1947. That year, the Dodgers won the National League **pennant**. Robinson was named National League Rookie of the Year.

The World Series

Often, the greatest baseball moments happen each year in October. That's when the World Series is played between the National and American League champions. Today, the World Series champions must win four out of seven possible games. It used to be eight. The first World Series was played in 1903. Boston beat Pittsburgh, five games to three.

One of the most popular moments in series history came in 2004 when the Boston Red Sox won their first World Series since 1918. According to **legend**, the great player, Babe Ruth, put a curse on the Red Sox when he left them to play with the New York Yankees. Fans say the curse was broken when the Red Sox beat the Yankees for the American League championship and went on to win the World Series.

Most Wins

The team with the most World Series championship wins is the New York Yankees. As of 20011, they had 27 wins. The team with the second-most wins is the St. Louis Cardinals with 11. The team that has gone the longest since a win is the Chicago Cubs, who last won in 1908.

The Red Sox came back from three games down to win the 2004 American League championship. No team had ever before come back from three games down in a championship series.

In the 1988 World Series, Kirk Gibson of the Los Angeles Dodgers hit a game-winning home run in the ninth inning. That win encouraged the Dodgers, and they won the World Series.

The Black Sox

Many people say that the worst moment in the history of the World Series came in 1919. That is when eight players from the Chicago White Sox were accused of **throwing** the series to the Cincinnati Reds. Although the players were cleared of committing a crime, they were banned from baseball for life. Because of their shame, the 1919 team has come to be known as the *Black Sox*.

Don Larsen pitched the only **perfect game** in World Series history, helping the Yankees to win the 1956 World Series, four games to three.

Little League

Baseball isn't just for adults! Kids everywhere love the game. Because of that, Carl Stotz began Little League Baseball in 1939 in Williamsport, Pennsylvania.

In Little League, teams play each other to learn about baseball, to practice good **sportsmanship**, and to compete for championships. At the end of each season, two teams from around the world compete in the Little League World Series. The first World Series was won by the Maynard Midgets of Williamsport.

At first, only boys were allowed in Little League. Beginning in 1974, girls were allowed to play. Then, in 1990, the Challenger Division for disabled children began. Today, there are thousands of Little League teams in 39 countries. Any child who wants to play can do so.

Thousands of former Little Leaguers have reached the Major Leagues, including Hall of Famers George Brett, Steve Carlton, Gary Carter, Rollie Fingers, Jim "Catfish" Hunter, Jim Palmer, Nolan Ryan, Mike Schmidt, Tom Seaver, Don Sutton, Carl Yastrzemski, and Robin Yount.

In 1947, Allen "Sonny" Yearick became the first former Little Leaguer to play professional baseball when he joined the Boston Braves.

In 1950, the first Little Leagues outside the United States were formed in Panama.

In the 1950s, a nine-year-old boy named George W. Bush began playing Little League. Years later, he would be the first former Little Leaguer to become president of the United States.

Did You Know?

The baseball song, "Take Me Out to the Ball Game," is one of the most popular songs in the United States. The words were written in 1908, and the music was written a little later. Surprisingly, the two men who wrote the song had never been to a baseball game!

Each year the Little League Baseball World Series is played in Williamsport, Pennsylvania.

Baseball Greats

Who are some of the greatest players in baseball history? Everyone has a different opinion. But most people can agree that the five players listed here are among the very best ever to play the game.

Babe Ruth—Ruth was one of the greatest home-run hitters of all time. He was the longtime holder of career- and single-season home-run records. He also held 12 American League home-run titles, four 50-homer seasons, six **RBI** titles, and a .342 career **batting average**.

Cy Young—Young was a great pitcher, and the pitching award given each year is named for him. He starred in the first World Series and had a career-record 511 wins, 7,356 innings pitched, and 749 complete games. He played for 22 seasons.

Hall of Fame

The National Baseball Hall of Fame opened in Cooperstown, New York, in 1939, to honor important people in the game of baseball. The first five players voted into the Hall of Fame were Ty Cobb, Babe Ruth, Honus Wagner, Walter Johnson, and Christy Mathewson. Now, more than 250 names have been added, as well as items such as the ball Babe Ruth hit for his 500th home run. Canada and Cuba also have halls of fame.

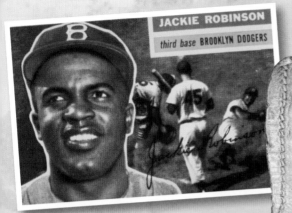

JACKIE ROBINSON
third base BROOKLYN DODGERS

Baseball Cards

Baseball cards show a player's picture and statistics. The first cards were made in the 1860s. Cards in the early 20th century often came packaged with gum or tobacco. Collecting baseball cards has been popular for a long time, and today it can even be big business.

Hank Aaron—One of the great home-run hitters, Hammerin' Hank played for 23 seasons and hit 755 home runs. In his career, he also had 3,771 hits, 2,174 runs scored, 2,297 RBIs, and a career .305 batting average. He was chosen to play in a record 25 **All-Star Games**.

Ted Williams—Williams played across 22 seasons, missing four years while away at war. During his playing time, he earned two **MVPs** (and just missed out on three more), six American League batting titles, 2,654 career hits, a .344 batting average, 19 All-Star Game invitations, and 521 home runs.

Willie Mays—Some people say that Mays was about as perfect as a baseball player could get. He is considered to be perhaps the greatest center fielder of all time and a great base runner, too. He was invited to 24 All-Star Games. He had a .302 career batting average. He played for 22 seasons, making 3,283 hits and 660 home runs.

Baseball Firsts

Baseball is full of famous firsts. Who stole the first base? Who hit the first **grand slam**? When did an announcer first say, "Going, going, gone!" when a home run flew over the fence? These and more famous firsts in baseball can be found in the time line on the next page.

Baseball Firsts Time Line

Eddie Cuthbert steals the first base.	**1865**
An umpire calls, "Play ball!" for the first time.	**1876**
Ross Barnes hits the first official home run.	**May 2, 1876**
George Bradley pitches the first no-hitter.	**July 15, 1876**
Players wear baseball gloves for the first time.	**1876**
The first schedule is made so that fans will know when their team is playing.	**1877**
Roger Connor hits the first official grand slam.	**Sept. 10, 1881**
There is corruption on record for the first time when an umpire cheats to fix a game.	**1882**
Moses Walker is the first African American player to play in a major league game.	**May 1, 1884**
The first World Series between the American and National Leagues is played.	**1903**
The first game is broadcast over the radio.	**Aug. 5, 1921**
Harry Hartman becomes the first announcer to say, "Going, going, gone!"	**1929**
The first night game is played.	**May 24, 1935**
Lou Gehrig is the first player to have his number retired.	**1939**

Glossary

All-Star Games—a game played once a year by the best players as voted on by the fans

amateur—someone who does a job but does not get paid for it

balk—a pitcher's illegal motion that suggests he will throw the ball but actually doesn't

barrier—a wall or obstruction

batting average—the number that says how often a batter gets a hit in relationship to the number of times the player goes to bat

cadet—a student at a military school

cricket—a British game resembling baseball played with bats, a ball, and wickets (upright stick targets)

forced out—caused to earn an out because the player has no safe base to run to

foul—occurs when the rules of a game are broken

grand slam—a home run hit when the bases are loaded so that four runs score

legend—a story handed down over time that many people believe to be true but cannot be proven

MVPs—Most Valuable Players

pennant—the championship of a league

perfect game—when a pitcher prevents any batters from reaching a base

professionals—people who do jobs and get paid for them, especially jobs that require special training or education to perform

pun—the humorous use of a word in such a way to suggest different meanings

RBI—Runs Batted In, or the number of runs a batter earns when players on base, including the batter, score because of the hit

rounders—a British game that resembles baseball

runs—points scored by crossing home plate safely after rounding all the bases

sportsmanship—good and fair behavior while playing a sport

standard—set or agreed upon

steal—occurs when a pitcher is about to throw the ball and a player at base runs to the next base before being caught

strikes—pitches thrown in the batter's strike zone and either swung on and missed by the batter or not swung on at all

throwing—losing intentionally

umpire—the judge in a baseball game

Index

About the Author

Dona Herweck Rice grew up in Anaheim, California, and graduated from the University of Southern California with a degree in English and from the University of California at Berkeley with a credential for teaching. She has been a teacher in preschool through tenth grade, a researcher, a librarian, and a theater director, and is now an editor, a poet, a writer of teacher materials, and a writer of books for children. She is married with two sons and lives in Southern California.